Original title:
Where Plants Whisper

Copyright © 2025 Creative Arts Management OÜ
All rights reserved.

Author: Aurora Sinclair
ISBN HARDBACK: 978-1-80581-805-2
ISBN PAPERBACK: 978-1-80581-332-3
ISBN EBOOK: 978-1-80581-805-2

Whispers in the Wilderness

In a garden full of leafy glances,
The tomatoes twirl in fruit-filled dances,
A mint plant giggles, how it fancies,
To tell the basil all its prances.

The carrots plot beneath the earth,
They throw a party for all they're worth,
Radishes rave about their girth,
While daisies roll around in mirth.

The ferns exchange their leafy jokes,
While sunflowers smile like clever folks,
Bees buzz in laughter, wings in strokes,
As nature's comic line provokes.

The oak stands tall, a serious guy,
Yet cracks a smile when squirrels fly by,
He can't believe how fast they try,
To catch a nut and then comply!

Echoes of Green

In the garden the veggies debate,
Carrots claim they're really great.
Tomatoes laugh, they're so red,
But parsley's quiet, tucked in bed.

Flowers giggle in colors bright,
Wondering who will win the fight.
Bees buzz in on secret flights,
Planning their honeyed delights.

Whispers Among Leaves

The daisies told secrets to the breeze,
While the daisies danced with such ease.
"Look at us, we're quite the show,"
"Don't forget who has the best row!"

A sunflower winked with pride at noon,
While dandelions hummed a tune.
"Did you hear the gossip, oh so spiffy?"
"Let's spill it all, it's blowin' shifty!"

The Language of Roots

Under the soil, whispers abound,
Roots telling tales that are quite profound.
A turnip yawned, "This soil's divine!"
While radishes boast, "We're all so fine!"

One little worm laughed at this pride,
"Down here, friends, I take a ride!"
They chuckled at the way they grew,
"Let's make this party a rooty brew!"

Beneath the Canopy

Under the trees, the squirrels convene,
Planning mischief that's quite obscene.
"Let's steal some acorns, then play a game,"
"Or challenge a bird, who's really to blame?"

In the shade, a frog jokes in rhyme,
Saying, "I hop better, give me some time!"
While mushrooms snicker in secret delight,
"Who knew being fungi could feel so light?"

Sweet Sounds of the Sapling

In the garden, leaves conspire,
Branches gossip, never tire.
A sapling sings a silly tune,
Bouncing joy like a balloon.

Worms do giggle, ants do dance,
Fluffy clouds join in the prance.
Sunshine tickles grass so bright,
Making shadows laugh in light.

Echoes from the Orchard

Apples chat with juicy pears,
Ripe bananas joke, no cares.
Cider dreams and fruity laughs,
Chortling under leafy swaths.

Bees buzz by with gossip grand,
While flowers cheer, a merry band.
Pomegranates burst with glee,
Tickled by a playful breeze.

The Quietude of Climbing Vines

Vines twist up, a tangled laugh,
Chasing sunlight, it's their path.
Laughing leaves in friendly fights,
Competing for the fluffiest heights.

Snails make bets on who climbs best,
While flowers giggle, quite impressed.
In their quiet, goes the joke,
As beetles join in on the poke.

Nocturne of the Nightshade

Underneath the moonlight's grace,
Nightshade humor finds its place.
Tall and dark, they share a jest,
Planning pranks that never rest.

With owls chuckling at the fun,
Crickets keep beat, never done.
A shadowed dance, a wink, a cheer,
Leaves unravel laughter here.

The Language of the Silent Flora

In the garden, blooms converse,
With petals fluttering, they disperse.
A rose told a joke, a daisy did laugh,
While tulips danced, a whimsical half.

The cacti grinned, all pokey and sly,
While ferns fanned gossip, oh my, oh my!
Sunflowers winked in the soft sunlight,
Bowing their heads, feeling just right.

Whispers of the Verdant Court

In a court of leaves, a trial did start,
The weeds filed in, each playing a part.
The judge was a bark, all wise and stout,
While violets argued, without a doubt.

The daisies petitioned for some more rain,
While grass said, "Nah, let's play in the grain!"
A peony whispered, in colorful tones,
"This garden's a riot; it's full of our bones!"

The Enchanted Garden's Tale

In an enchanted plot, all green and sweet,
The carrots laughed loud, in their underground seat.
The radishes showed off their roots with pride,
While basil thought it'd be fun to hide.

The mint threw a party, got everyone high,
With laughter and herbs, oh my, oh my!
But violets who peeked, said, "That's not so fair,
We're stuck here in soil, we need more air!"

Beneath the Rustling Green

Beneath the leaves, the laughter flows,
A playful breeze makes the petals chose.
The mushrooms giggle, all snug in their place,
While ivy attempts to join in the race.

The broccoli waltzed, looking so neat,
With radishes teetering on their tiny feet.
The daisies rolled over, all heads in a whirl,
"Next time," they said, "let's ask for a twirl!"

Soft Voices of the Leafy Sentinels

In the garden, leaves do chat,
Gossiping about the fat old cat.
"Did you see that squirrel's wild dash?"
"I thought for sure he'd make a splash!"

The daisies wink at passing bees,
Telling tales of the soft spring breeze.
"Watch out for that clumsy fellow!"
"He's so confused, his head's a jello!"

The Wisdom of the Wild

Moss gives advice on how to chill,
"Just roll with it, and eat your fill!"
The ferns nod wisely, green and spry,
Even they laugh when an acorn flies!

Old oaks claim to know the best jokes,
While quacking ducks just chuckle and poke.
"Why did the tree cross the road?"
"To branch out, buddy! Here's the code!"

Songs of Nature's Embrace

Crickets chirp a tune so bright,
While snoozing snails join in the night.
"I'm not slow," one smugly hums,
"I'm just conserving; here it comes!"

The flowers sway—oh, what a show!
"Dance like no one's watching, go!"
Bees buzz harmonies, friends unite,
"Just don't step on me—ouch, that's tight!"

Hushed Secrets of the Wilds

In shady corners, secrets spread,
Toadstools giggle, "He's lost his head!"
A chattering robin swings on a line,
"Did you hear that? He's still on time!"

Bamboo whispers, sly and low,
"Hurry up, dude, let's put on a show!"
With all these whispers, how can you sleep?
"Naptime's for later; let's hear the peep!"

Secrets in the Soil

The potatoes giggle, buried deep,
Do they dream of fries or just want to sleep?
The carrots gossip of their orange fame,
While radishes blush, all too shy to claim.

A worm in a tux, ready for the ball,
Doing the cha-cha, having a ball.
Soil's a banquet of wormy delight,
Dancing to tunes that last through the night.

Murmurs of the Meadow

In the grass, a rabbit throws a rave,
Inviting the crickets, wild and brave.
The daisies sway, trying to keep pace,
While the breeze chats up the daisies' lace.

Bees bumble in with a raucous hum,
Critiquing the flowers, 'You need more yum!'
A butterfly flutters, wings in a swirl,
As the butterflies argue who's the best girl.

Tales of the Treetops

A squirrel spins tales of acorn heists,
While branches shake as the wind entices.
The crows crack jokes, leaning on a limb,
While leaves just rustle, shrugging at whim.

A woodpecker pecks out a funny beat,
Telling the tale of his snazzy feat.
And a sleepy owl, in his comfy nook,
Loses the punchline—he just wants to look.

Born from Gentle Breezes

The flowers giggle when the wind sings,
Whispering secrets about all sorts of things.
The lilacs chuckle, thinking they're bold,
While daisies gossip, their petals unfold.

A dandelion dreams of being a star,
Blowing wishes whispered near and far.
The breeze joins in with a playful swirl,
Crafting the tales of each twirl and whirl.

Sway of the Serene

In a meadow, flowers dance,
They twirl and giggle, take a chance.
A dandelion sneezes, oh dear!
The bees all chuckle, full of cheer.

The trees wear hats, made of green,
They gossip softly, unseen, serene.
A squirrel passes, with a nut so round,
And laughter echoes all around.

The grass has tickles, oh so sly,
As ants march by in a tidy line.
A ladybug winks, thinks it's sly,
Says, "Catch me if you can, oh my!"

So in this garden full of glee,
Nature's humor runs wild and free.
Each petal sings a little song,
In this delight, we all belong.

The Quiet Thrumming

Amidst the foliage, frogs conspire,
Strumming their tunes, never tire.
With leafy blankets, they do sing,
A chorus set for napping spring.

The worms, they wiggle, quite bemused,
In the dirt disco, they're infused.
Eggshells clink like brittle glass,
While moss forms hills, a soft green mass.

The wind joins in, with a whistle clear,
A playful touch as it brushes near.
Each blade of grass has jokes to share,
In the hush, finds laughter everywhere.

And when the day softens its glow,
Nature's secret giggles overflow.
In the quiet, the world still hums,
Where jest and joy are never done.

Embrace of the Earth

In the corners where shadows play,
Bunnies hop in a silly way.
With carrots tucked behind their ears,
They bounce and jingle, bring on cheers.

The sunflowers nod with grinning faces,
As little bugs parade in races.
"Don't step on me!" the daisies cry,
While butterflies swirl through the sky.

A hedgehog rolls when pricked with glee,
Trying to hide behind a tree.
The world's a stage, where laughter lifts,
Notes of joy, the universe gifts.

Here, life's a jest, and all partake,
In the warmth of love, we gently shake.
Within the earth's great, funny mirth,
Joy springs forth, an endless birth.

Stories in the Shadows

In the twilight, whispers bloom,
Crickets chirp, dispelling gloom.
The mushrooms gather for a chat,
"Is that a beetle? No, it's a cat!"

In knots of roots, the tales are spun,
Of brave little bugs who loved to run.
With tiny swords made of sharp grass,
They battle weeds that dare to pass.

The moon peeks in with a twinkling grin,
As fireflies join the merry din.
"Is that the wind, or a joking ghost?"
Leaves rustle, the shadow folks boast.

So wander here, let laughter reign,
In secret spots where dreams entertain.
In every twist, a small surprise,
As nature shares her funny lies.

A Tapestry of Quietude

In the garden, the tulips dance,
Stretching limbs as if in trance.
They gossip softly, petals sway,
Plotting pranks to brighten the day.

The ivy winks, a twinkle bright,
Confesses to the moon at night.
With clever vines, it weaves a tale,
Of snickering roses that never fail.

A cactus chuckles, spine quite sharp,
Playing tunes on a leaf-shaped harp.
While daisies giggle, full of cheer,
Competing for the sun, oh dear!

And so they sing, this leafy crew,
Chasing squirrels, jumping through dew.
In every leaf, a secret told,
In every bud, a joke unfolds.

Whispers in the Wilderness

A dandelion, with fluff and flair,
Reveals a truth, or maybe a dare.
It puffs and laughs, releasing seeds,
Spreading giggles, like little weeds.

The ferns are busy, plotting the scene,
Gossiping about the beans and greens.
With leaves that rustle in humorous spree,
They're the best kept giggle therapy.

Mossy patches, with faces so sly,
Hide little critters who peek and spy.
They swap and share the wildest dreams,
With laughter echoing through the streams.

Amidst the trees, a woodpecker knocks,
Making fun of the old tree's socks.
Nature's fun, where laughter will sprout,
When roots start talking, there's no doubt.

Secrets of the Sage

In the herb patch, the thyme takes bets,
On which worm will win the daily sets.
With whispers shared in leafy corners,
They plan antics with nature's mourners.

The sage, wise and full of jest,
Speaks in riddles, life's funny quest.
While the basil twirls, with a wink,
Says, 'Life's too short to really think!'

Chives stir up a fragrant tease,
Chasing the breezes with effortless ease.
While lemon balm, with a giggly tone,
Reveals secrets of weather not known.

In this garden, humor abounds,
With each leafy laugh, joy surrounds.
Nature's comedy, a fragrant parade,
With every herb, a joke's been made.

The Garden's Lullaby

At dusk, the daisies start to yawn,
Whispering tales of the sleepy dawn.
With petals drooping, they share a doze,
And trade soft giggles, nobody knows.

The carrots giggle underground,
Telling tales without a sound.
Awake under moonlight, they plot a game,
While radishes roll, teasing their name.

The snails tell stories, oh so slow,
Of races they've lost, in the row below.
But they chuckle and shrug, with sweet delight,
'Tomorrow's another chance, let's take flight!'

Moonbeams dance on leaves and stems,
As laughter flickers like firefly gems.
In this garden, dreams come alive,
As each silly jest helps the night thrive.

The Graces of Greenery

In a garden full of dreams,
The daisies plot with schemes.
They giggle when the roses pout,
And whisper secrets, sweet and stout.

The ferns dance with leafy flair,
While the weeds just steal their air.
A sunflower winks, quite bold,
While tall grass shares tales of old.

A gnome then joins the leafy crew,
Spying on the bugs that flew.
The cucumbers conspire with glee,
About world domination, you see!

But when the garden gets too loud,
The mushrooms sit beneath a cloud.
With jokes that make the soil shake,
They laugh till all the flowers break!

Sighs of the Shrubs

In a hedge, the secrets sway,
The bushes sigh throughout the day.
One bush claims it saw a cat,
The other swears it knew a bat.

With twisted branches, tales they weave,
Of starlit nights and bits of thieves.
The lilacs whisper, soft and bright,
About the bugs that stole their light.

They grumble when the rain arrives,
And start their gossip—oh, the jives!
The hawthorn winks, a clever sage,
"Did you hear? It's bee-sized rage!"

In the shade, the shadows dance,
Nutmeg plants take their chance.
As thorns provide their prickly jest,
They find that chaos is the best!

Beneath the Blossoms

Beneath the blooms, a green brigade,
Plays hide and seek in leafy shade.
The poppies giggle, tulips chime,
While bumblebees perfect their rhyme.

With petals soft, the daffodils,
Trade silly jokes and little thrills.
A ladybug, quite cheeky and spry,
Claims she flew up to the sky!

The crocus cracks a smile so wide,
With jokes about how worms can hide.
And whenever the wind starts to play,
They all sway and shout, "Hip Hip Hooray!"

But once the sun begins to set,
They tell tall tales you won't forget.
For under blooms, 'neath stars so bright,
Silly whispers fill the dark night!

Soft Rustle, Soft Heart

In the meadow, laughter flows,
Rustling leaves in playful rows.
Nature's choir hums a tune,
While crickets dance beneath the moon.

The willow waves with gentle grace,
Telling tales of a snail's race.
"Slow and steady wins the day,"
Chortles a squirrel in full display.

Then flowers giggle, heads held high,
As dandy lions flirt and sigh.
The violets claim they're royalty,
While jumping jacks prance joyfully.

The night wraps all in soft embrace,
As rustles start the dreamy chase.
Beneath the stars, hearts twirl and spin,
In this garden where laughs begin!

The Lullaby of the Forest

In a wood where trees do nap,
Squirrels gossip, take a lap.
Fungi giggle, clowns of the ground,
Mice tell tales, funny sounds.

The owls hoot in sleepy jest,
Bears in pajamas, oh what a quest.
All the leaves clap in delight,
As the sun bids goodnight.

Branches stretch like yawning folk,
Breezes chuckle, tickle and poke.
Mushrooms dance on their little toes,
As the evening laughter grows.

Moonlight spills like spilled milk,
The forest grins, soft as silk.
And in this wacky, leafy spree,
Nature's jokes are wild and free!

Quiet Counsel of the Undergrowth

In the thickets, chatty vines,
Bumblebees draw funny lines.
Grasses wave like little hands,
Plotting jokes with silly bands.

Twirling roots with secrets tight,
Caterpillars dance in delight.
Toads croak out the punchlines clear,
While the crickets clap and cheer.

A wise old tree, with knots and scars,
Tells the rumors of the stars.
He whispers low, with a cheeky grin,
As ferns play tag and softly spin.

Calm shadows cast their playful scenes,
Nature's giggles reign supreme.
Silly sounds among the green,
In a world where smiles are seen!

Whispers from the Sagebrush

Beyond the cacti, oh what a sight,
Sagebrush chuckles in the moonlight.
Lizards wiggle, trying to dance,
While tumbleweeds take a chance.

Crickets hold a nightly quiz,
Rabbits hop in a lively fizz.
Yuccas roll their eyes, so coy,
While the desert hums with joy.

Cacti wear hats made from dew,
Sharing punchlines, jokes anew.
In the darkness, giggles sweep,
As the stars in the sky peep.

In this realm of sand and brush,
Nature's laughter fills the hush.
Every whisper, every jest,
Is a playful nature's quest!

The Chronicles of Green Shadows

Underneath the leafy crown,
Shadows dance, never a frown.
Creepy-crawlies in a play,
Sock puppets made of hay.

Chirping frogs on lily pads,
Making faces, oh such lads.
As the bugs join in the fun,
Frogs leap high, seeking the sun.

The willows sway, shaking their heads,
As silly gnomes swap their beds.
Leaves whisper tales of mischief done,
In a world so bright and fun!

The woods echo with giggles sweet,
Every creature tapping their feet.
A feast of laughter in the night,
Where green shadows shine so bright!

Secrets of the Silent Grove

In the shade, the weeds conspire,
To outgrow the grass, they all aspire.
A dandelion wears a crown so grand,
While daisies dance and try to stand.

Trees giggle as they sway,
Telling tales of the rogue raccoon's play.
The mushrooms hold their secret meet,
Sharing whispers of tasty feet.

Frogs croak jests from their leafy thrones,
While squirrels steal acorns, claiming them as their own.
The breeze carries laughter, soft and light,
As the garden's party goes on all night.

In this grove, the humor burbles,
With every petal and vine, it curdles.
A snail tells jokes, slow and dry,
While butterflies flutter, rolling their eyes high.

Echoes Beneath the Canopy

Under leaves, the chitter-chatter,
Of beetles and bugs, in laughter they patter.
A wise old oak shakes its head with glee,
As it listens to gossip from the ivy spree.

The ferns gossip in swaying frames,
While blossoms giggle at silly names.
A cricket gets the crowd in stitches,
With tales of crafting muddy ditches.

The sunflower winks, with a nod to the moon,
As shadows play their silly tune.
Balloons of pollen float like dreams,
In this canopy of whimsical schemes.

Even the roots below can't refrain,
From sharing jokes about the rain.
Each sip of dew a giggling potion,
Making nature's humor a funny notion.

Conversations in the Green

In the patch where colors burst,
A daisy claimed it was the first.
"I was here before the sun awoke!"
And giggled as a passing bee bespoke.

A tomato blushed from a fun little tease,
While carrots cracked jokes with all the ease.
"I'm not a fruit!" the berry would shout,
As cucumbers rolled, having no doubt.

The wind joins in with tickling sighs,
Whispering sweetly through busy lives.
They share funny stories of the big rain,
And laugh at the puddles left in their plain.

Here in the green where all things bounce,
Nature's humor makes hearts trounce.
With every rustle, the fun never ends,
As laughter echoes among all the friends.

Murmurs of the Leafy Realm

Whispers flutter among the tall grass,
While ants organize a dance to outlast.
A butterfly jokes of needing caffeine,
While one little roach dreams of being seen.

The willow creaks with a chuckle and sway,
"I'm the shadiest one, what do you say?"
The herbs laugh at a weed's clumsy flip,
As the fence posts join in for a cartoonish quip.

Petunias gossip about the morning dew,
While the sunflowers wave, "Aren't we cute too?"
Rabbits pause to hear the green tales unfold,
Of hilarious squirrels and bold potpourri old.

Every rustle and murmur in the leafy range,
Paints a scene that'll never change.
With giggles and tittering, they lighten the air,
In the realm of green, there's laughter to share.

Echoes in Eden

In a garden full of beans,
The flowers burst into scenes,
Rabbits dance with glee,
While ants sip their tea.

The tomatoes wear silly hats,
As cucumbers share their chats,
Gazing at the sky,
Wishing they could fly!

A bee spins a funny tale,
About a snail who's gone pale,
He claimed he saw a ghost,
But it was just a host!

With laughter floating high,
The plants wave goodbye,
In echoes of delight,
A whimsical night!

The Hidden Harmony

In the shade, the mushrooms sing,
Creating joy from little things,
A squirrel plays the flute,
While a mole dons a suit.

The daisies hold a dance,
As the crickets start to prance,
With hiccups loud and bright,
They sway into the night.

The roots start to crack a joke,
Making the soil laugh and choke,
As the carrots do a jig,
And the snap peas grow big!

With nature's giggling spree,
Even weeds join the glee,
In harmony so sweet,
A comedic retreat!

A Chorus of Chlorophyll

The ferns are swaying in a line,
Singing songs made of sunshine,
With a wink and a grin,
They reel the lilies in.

Two cacti share a goofy tease,
Telling tales of bumblebees,
While sunflowers march with pride,
In hats that swing side to side.

With leaves that flutter and sway,
They turn night into day,
The vines twist in a whirl,
As the morning glories twirl!

In a chorus all around,
Laughter is profound,
In greens, it's clear to see,
Nature's comedy!

Symphonies of the Soil

A cacophony of green and brown,
Where worms wear crowns like a clown,
The daisies laugh in lines,
While mint plays on the vines.

The beetles tap-dance on the leaves,
Building beats as the garden weaves,
With whispers soft and low,
Their funny dreams still grow.

The radishes have crazy plans,
And chat with grinning pans,
As the lettuce teases shy,
"Join in, don't be so dry!"

With soil's symphony in tune,
Under the chuckling moon,
In every nook and cranny,
Nature's humor runs uncanny!

The Hush of Ferns

In leafy silence they conspire,
Ferns gossip low—who needs a choir?
The sun takes notes, the shadows laugh,
As droplets dance on their green staff.

One claims to hold the best of shade,
While another boasts of being unafraid.
Watch them swish in a leafy twirl,
A jungle flash mob, in a verdant whirl.

The squirrel sneaks by, a judge so sly,
He nods and winks, can't let time fly.
With each soft sneeze from the breezy swarm,
Both tease the winds, oh what a charm!

As night descends, they let out a cheer,
For the moon's soft glow brings stories near.
In the hush of ferns, all is well,
Nature's humor, weaves a spell.

Echoing in the Underbrush

Beneath the shrubs, a raucous crew,
Bugs and critters, join in too.
They crack jokes about the moon's big grin,
While dodging raindrops, a merry din.

The raccoon's tales, so wild and bold,
Of nighttime snacks, worth their weight in gold.
A rabbit chimes in, with a cheeky jest,
"Life's just a race, I'm the very best!"

Even the twigs seem to snicker,
As the lazy cat naps and gets thicker.
What's that noise, a thump, a thud?
Oh just the groundhog, making a bud!

In this silly mix of rustling fray,
Laughter carries the night away.
As dawn peeks in, the echoes stay,
In the underbrush, they'll always play.

Conversations with the Wind

The breeze tickles trees, oh such fun,
Chasing the leaves, just on the run.
"Catch me if you can!" it taunts and plays,
While squirrels pause, in amazed gaze.

"Did you hear that?" whispers a branch,
"Seems the wind's got a new romance!"
With rustling leaves, they share a grin,
Can you believe the stories spin?

The wind spends tales, of clouds and sun,
Of playful storms that never shun.
"I'm a highs and lows kind of friend,"
Whistles in joy, "Let the laughter blend!"

So here they chatter, both light and spry,
Where whispers dance and worries die.
In every gust, a chuckle we find,
With every whiff, joys entwined.

Wisdom of the Wildflowers

Wildflowers gather, all in a row,
Swapping secrets, delightfully slow.
"Did you smell that breeze? Smells like a plan!"
They giggle, as petals swirl in the span.

"Could we get fame with our bright display?"
One sunflower beams, in a bright array.
A daisy chuckles, "Oh please, my friend,
It's our charm that will always transcend!"

With a rustle here, and a sway from there,
They whisper 'bout bees, that zoom and dare.
"Remember that time we made them spin?
They looked so puzzled, where to begin?"

As night draws close, the laughter stays,
In a patch of color, creating rays.
The wisdom blooms, in giggles galore,
Nature's humor, forever to adore.

Murmurs of Mist

In a garden with glee, the flowers play,
Telling secrets to bees, all night and day.
They giggle and sway, tickling the air,
In their leafy gossip, they haven't a care.

The sun tries to listen, but it's way too bright,
While shadows in corners share stories at night.
The daisies tease roses, 'You think you're so grand!'
But the violets just laugh, with a wink and a hand.

A squirrel named Pete joins the chatter below,
He spills all the beans on the things he knows.
Each leaf holds a joke, and laughter's the tune,
Amid the soft rustles, an orchestra's boon.

With whispers and chuckles, the plants stay spry,
They dance in the breeze, letting giggles fly.
The garden's a comedy, oh what a scene!
In this green, leafy realm, all's silly and keen!

The Swaying Song

The branches are jiving, leaves shimmy with zest,
Every rustle and flap, a nature's big fest.
The daisies hum tunes as they dance in a row,
While the ferns sway so high, like they're putting on a show.

The wind's got the rhythm, it sweeps through the trees,
Tickling the stems with a soft, gentle tease.
"Hey, look at that clover, it's doing a flip!"
And a nearby sunflower does the worm with a dip.

As bouncy as popcorn, the petals rejoice,
With whispers like giggles, they all share one voice.
Each twig and each leaf has a story to share,
In this lively ballet, they float through the air.

So come join the fun, let the laughter extend,
In this garden of chatter, where all are a friend.
With humor in blossoms, let's dance with delight,
In this swaying, merry, green world—oh, what a sight!

The Gentle Touch of Tendrils

Sneaky little tendrils, reaching for fun,
Tickle the petals, oh what a run!
With a twist and a turn, they giggle and tease,
Creeping up lightly with such graceful ease.

"Hey, buddy, you there, what's your favorite leaf?"
A vine whispers softly, "I like them in sheaf!"
With a grin that can bloom, they share all around,
In the world of the green, laughter's unbound.

The ivy will brag about climbing so high,
While the orchids just flutter, "You can't catch the sky!"
With a flicker of humor, they wrap 'round and play,
In this tangled-up comedy, a leafy ballet.

So let's plant ourselves here, among whispers and cheer,
Where tendrils are teasing, no need for a leer.
In this garden of giggles, wrapped up tight,
The gear of good humor spins day and night!

Sheltered Secrets

Beneath a broad leaf, there's chatter and chit,
Where the tiny green critters all gather and sit.
The roses blush pink as they gossip and grieve,
"Do you think it's too soon for the spring to leave?"

In the cool shaded nook where the mushrooms convene,
They swap spooky stories, both silly and mean.
A beetle pipes up, "Have you seen my new ride?"
"It's shiny and quick, but my shell is my pride!"

They plot little pranks, like a jester's delight,
Rolling acorns like marbles, oh what a sight!
While the daisies conspire about who's in bloom,
They hide all the laughter away from the gloom.

In this whimsical place, beneath leaves they can chat,
Their whispers afloat like a soft, gentle mat.
So here in this shelter, let the secrets unfold,
A garden of humor, with stories retold.

Voices of the Verdant

Beneath the leafy canopy, a chat so spry,
The daisies gossip sweetly, as bees zoom by.
A cactus boasts of size, swaying with proud might,
While orchids roll their eyes in the soft moonlight.

A dandelion sneezes, 'Oh watch out, beware!'
The tulips laugh together, their petals in the air.
The ferns are feathered dancers, in a swift ballet,
With roots that tickle squirrels as they hop and play.

The sunflowers pose like models, in the bright sun's glow,

Trying to find the best angle for their show.
The lilacs throw a party, inviting all their friends,
They sing, they sway, and hope the laughter never ends.

But don't forget the weeds, with their wild, woeful ways,
They crash the bloom fest early, igniting plant malaise.
Yet laughter fills the garden, in every nook and bend,
For here, among the greenery, there's always room to mend.

Hushed Harmony

In the shadows of the shrubs, a secret's softly spun,
The ivies giggle gently, 'Oh, what a silly pun!'
The lilting of the lilies, in whispers as they sway,
Turns every silent moment into something light and gay.

The moss holds court with whispers from below,
While toadstools tell tall tales, just putting on a show.
The twinkling stars above tap dance with roots so wise,
In a frolicsome ballet beneath the moonlit skies.

The roses boast of colors, all dazzling and bold,
While the shyest of the violets just softly glow, not cold.
The daisies cut the tension, with jokes about the sun,
While branches join their laughter, for they're all here for fun!

Yet when the gardener comes near, there's a hush of care,
The plants all freeze in laughter, hiding everywhere.
And when the coast is clear, they erupt with gleeful cheer,

In this secret leafy world, every giggle draws us near.

Breaths of the Briar

In the thicket of the brambles, a jester's jest takes flight,
The nettles poke and prod while the thorns hold on tight.
The hedgehogs hold their breath, unsure of what's to come,
While the weeds roll in the grass, twirling just for fun.

The willow bends to listen, what secrets do they tell?
The whispers of the wild ones are truly quite the spell.
A thistle shrieks with laughter, 'Oh give it all you've got!'

While the roses shake their heads, declaring, 'Not a lot!'

But as the sun shines down, the leaves begin to sway,
They conjure up a chorus, in a foliage ballet.
The dew drops join the fun, they glisten and they gleam,
Choreographing giggles, like nature's crazy dream.

But then the winds come howling, oh such a fickle friend,

The brambles brace for trouble, as the laughter starts to bend.
Yet in this wild, bristly world, the humor stays alive,
For even in the thorns, the joy begins to thrive.

The Song of Sprouts

Tiny sprouts in a huddle, all green and full of cheer,
Debating on the weather: 'Is it winter? Is it near?'
The radishes insist, 'We surely need a snack!'
While the beans plot their climb, with the chirping in the back.

One sunflower declares, 'Let's start a talent show!'
While peas roll on the ground, crafting snowballs made of dough.
The carrots form a band, with leaves as their guitars,
Strumming tunes of laughter beneath the glow of stars.

A beet bursts with excitement, 'I'm the root of all the fun!'

While sprouts tell silly stories, 'Oh, remember when we'd run?'
The radishes now tumble, in a playful, silly spree,
While turnips cheer them on, with their tops all frolicy.

But as the clouds roll in, the sprouts chew on their fate,
'Will we be splashed in rain? Or just get stuck and wait?'
Yet through the whims of nature, their giggles fill the air,
For every sprout knows laughter is the best of nature's care.

Soliloquy of Sunlight

Sunshine gleams on grassy blades,
Tickling leaves in sunny parades.
'Hey there, daisies, look at me,
I'm the star of this garden spree!'

Butterflies dance in leafy delight,
'Is that a flower or a dress so bright?'
'Nope, just me, keeping things light,
Wearing petals, what a sunny sight!'

Caterpillars munch, all quite sly,
'We'll be butterflies, oh my, oh my!'
As bees buzz in their busy throng,
'Just wait and see, we'll all sing along!'

And thus the sunlight carries on,
Creating laughter till the day is gone.

Conversations in the Compost

In the heap where leftovers go,
Vegetables chat, 'What a show!
Peelings, cores, don't feel so sad,
We're here for a future that's not half bad!'

'Oh, look at us, we're breaking down,
Turning into nutrients for the crown.'
'Yes, grand tomatoes will take our place,
We're the secret to their leafy grace!'

A worm winks, 'I'm the real star here,
Dining on scraps, with hearty cheer!'
Lettuce leaves shriek, 'Not too close!'
Worm love's all mushy, that's a real boast!'

So in the muck, they find their glee,
Nature's comedy, just wait and see!

Beneath the Boughs

Under branches big and round,
Squirrels chatter, jumping around.
'Is that a nut or just bad luck?
I swear I saw it, but now I'm stuck!'

A crow caws high, 'You silly little things,
Chasing dreams like they've got wings!'
'Stop it, bird, and lend an ear,
We're just executing nutty fear!'

Leaves giggle softly, swaying with sass,
'You think you're quick? Just wait, you grass!'
The grass replies, 'You're all so rude,
But I'll grow proud, and be in the mood!'

Beneath the boughs, chaos reigns supreme,
A world of laughter, a leafy dream.

Soft Echoes of Elms

Whispers float on a gentle breeze,
'Hey, root friends, it's time to tease!'
'Can you feel this tickle below?
Just don't ask the soil—it's in the know!'

Crickets chirp, 'Shhh, listen close,
We'll make music, it's what we boast!'
Grasshoppers laugh, 'With legs so long,
Hop along, we'll sing our song!'

A gnarled tree sighs, 'I'm wise and old,
Tell us a story, some secrets untold!'
'Listen up, I've seen it all,
From tiny seeds to the grand tree ball!'

And so they chatter, all day through,
Nature's giggle in the morning dew.

Echoes Through the Thorns

In a garden filled with needles,
Gossipy bushes lose their steeples.
The roses chuckle, petals flail,
As thorns stab jokes like a fierce whale.

A daisy winks at passing bees,
Says, 'Watch out for the sneezing trees!'
Mint frolics in a leafy dance,
While tangerines share a flamboyant prance.

Lettuce jokes about a salad's fate,
It dreams of grandeur, feeling quite great.
But when it's tossed, it lets out a cry,
"Why does my life end in a pie?"

So join this banter, silly and bright,
Where every herb is a comedian's delight.
As roots tangle, they cackle with glee,
In this patch, everyone's funny to see!

Conversations with the Wind-Swept Blades

The grass is lively, whispering jest,
Tickling toes that dare to rest.
It sways and swirls, a green parade,
Laughing at troubles, like a charade.

'Look at the daisies, blooming in style!
With their sunny hats, they walk a mile.'
Said the weeds, in their haphazard fashion,
Yet, they laugh with a twinge of passion.

A tree with branches seems to nod,
'What's with the flowers acting so odd?'
While wilted petals sigh in despair,
'Oh, the sun doesn't seem to care!'

So the grass chuckles, sharing the tease,
While squirrels dance like they own the trees.
In this green realm where silliness sways,
Even the roots tell jokes in their ways!

Beneath the Quiet Canopy

Beneath the leaves, the shadows play,
Moss giggles softly, oh, what a fray!
A mushroom jokes, 'I'm a fun-guy too,'
While clovers are cheering, 'Who knew? Who knew?'

The ferns sway gently, in rhythmic cheer,
Whispering secrets for all to hear.
'Look at us wiggle!' they say with a grin,
'Whatever you do, don't let us spin!'

A squirrel overheard, twitched its cute nose,
'They're just jealous 'cause nobody knows,
How much I stash—nuts galore!
If they could, they'd ask for just one more!'

So giggle in shade, let hilarity ring,
Among the green, where laughter takes wing.
For even the trees sway with delight,
In this playful haven, oh what a sight!

The Enigma of the Emerald Shadows

In emerald depths, shadows debate,
Is it just green, or is it first-rate?
The flowers giggle, casting their votes,
While sunlight frets, trying on coats.

'Why wear yellow?' the lilies exclaim,
'Green's the real star, never the same!'
A snapdragon snorts, 'Let's stay a bit shy,
My petals are posh, but don't judge my dye!'

A breeze jogs by, too cool for the shade,
'Guys, let's stop—these hues need a trade!'
As tall grass whispers, 'I think we should swap,
What's the harm in a color flip-flop?'

So beneath the emerald, shadows unite,
Creating a canvas of laughter and light.
For each little quirk adds to the charm,
In this leafy laughter, there's no cause for alarm!

Requiem of the Reeds

In the bend of the marsh, reeds stand tall,
They gossip all day, never a dull call.
They swish and they sway, in the breeze they play,
Whispering secrets in a green ballet.

A frog hops by and with a grin,
He asks the reeds to let the rumors in.
With laughter, they sway, in dramatic display,
"Did you see the duck? He slipped on his way!"

The dragonflies buzz, spouting such jokes,
About snapping turtles and curious folks.
With giggles and snorts, the reeds hold court,
Making merry tales from their little resort.

So here's to the reeds, with quirky delight,
Their humor and sass, a real fun insight.
In laughter they bloom, in sunshine they zoom,
A watery world where the wild hearts loom.

The Soft Dance of Delicate Petals

Petals twirl round in a fanciful waltz,
Laughing at raindrops that spill with no faults.
They tickle the breeze, with colors so bright,
Giggling at clouds, what a comical sight!

The windy trickster comes by for a tease,
Pulling on petals like teasing a sneeze.
"Catch me if you can!" they flutter and flit,
As bees buzz around in a fidgety fit.

A butterfly stops, with a curious face,
Says, "Mind if I join in this giggly race?"
Together they spin, oh what joyful cheer,
Making merry mischief, spreading good cheer.

So dance, little petals, in sunlight's embrace,
With each windy turn, the world's a fun place.
In the soft dance of spring, with laughter they spring,
Nature's own carnival, where giggles take wing.

Timeless Tales of Timber

Old oaks creak back, sharing stories of yore,
Of squirrels who planned grand heists for some more.
"Remember the time," the branches all chuckle,
When a nut thief was chased, nearly lost his buckle!

The bark holds the tales, both silly and wise,
Of the raccoon who thought he was winning a prize.
Climbed to the top, but oh what a plight,
He got stuck up there till the fall of the night.

Then came a woodpecker, tapping with flair,
"Need help, my friend, for you're quite in despair!"
With a wink and a laugh, they all made a fuss,
Soon joined by the chipmunk, who rode on a bus!

So gather 'round trees, let's share a good laugh,
With immeasurable tales in this woodland staff.
Timber's own legacy, both wild and free,
A jolly old gathering of bark and glee.

Laughter of the Blossoms

In the garden of giggles, the blossoms are bright,
They chatter and chuckle with pure delight.
"Did you hear the joke?" a daisy does say,
"About the sunflower who got lost on her way?"

The tulips, they're snickering, leaning quite close,
Sporting all colors, they laugh and they boast.
With petals flapping, they play peek-a-boo,
"Oh, let's not blush, we look fabulous too!"

The wind carries tales, whispering by fast,
Of bees doing ballet, in pollen they're cast.
From rose to the lily, the laughter does bloom,
In this cheeky garden, there's never a gloom.

So frolic, dear flowers, and fill up the air,
With humor and joy, free as love without care.
In the laughter of blossoms, magic does spin,
A riot of color, let the fun times begin!

The Silence of Succulents

In the corner sits a prickly mate,
Who thinks he's just so really great.
With a smug little grin, he waves at the sun,
While giggling plants think it's all a ton of fun.

Cacti grumble, their needles a tease,
'We need more water, yet we simply freeze!'
A leafy laughter rises from pots,
As they plot who will steal the gardener's thoughts.

Every leaf whispers, in secret delight,
'We're the true rulers of this quiet site!'
Succulents snicker, hiding their glee,
As they play games in their green jubilee.

One little fern dared to jiggle about,
While roots conspired, creating a rout.
In the shade of the sun, they dance with grace,
These cheeky greens claim their own special space.

Voices in the Verdant Umbra

In the shade of leaves, secrets unfold,
With whispers of tales, daring and bold.
The ivy rolls its eyes, quite unimpressed,
While the daisies laugh, in floral jest.

'Oh, have you met the rock that's so chill?'
It dared the roots to climb up the hill.
'While we bask under stars, won't it be grand?
To gossip with moss, across the green land!'

A worm overhears and wiggles with glee,
'Your gossip is juicy, come tell it to me!'
But the daisies wink, with a nod and a grin,
'Our secrets are safe, let the fun begin!'

In the twilight shade, they share all the news,
As laughter erupts in their verdant shoes.
Even the grass has a ticklish sway,
In the voices of green that mix night and day.

Petals in the Breeze

Petals flutter, like whispers in flight,
Blowing stories beneath the soft light.
While bees buzz in rhythm, in sweet disarray,
The flowers conspire, 'Let's have a play!'

A rose claims the crown, with a royal flair,
While daisies chant, 'We don't care! We don't care!'
With a hop and a skip, they dance through the air,
In a floral fiesta, with laughs everywhere.

But the sunflowers laugh, stretching way too tall,
'We see it all; we can touch the wall!'
While tulips toss petals like confetti in cheer,
Colorful giggles spread far and near.

Amidst the sweet scents, joy blooms in the breeze,
Where petals converse and tickle the trees.
With laughter in whispers, they share their delight,
These flowered friends dancing under the night.

Ebb and Flow of Green Harmony

In a pot where vines twist and twine,
Each leaf whispers secrets, oh so fine.
As the ferns sway gently, tipping in time,
They sing silly songs, no rhythm or rhyme.

The clover chuckles, with a four-leafed grin,
'Perhaps one of us might earn a win!'
While daisies declare, with a twankly shout,
'Let's spread joy like petals, without a doubt!'

The fussy orchids frown, but can't help but cheer,
'You silly green things, there's nothing to fear!'
For in this green world, where laughter flows free,
Life's a whimsical tune of botanical glee.

So they sway and they spin, in their leafy ballet,
Spreading bright vibes in a jazzy array.
With roots that connect, through the soil and the dew,
In the ebb and flow, they're one big green crew!

Shadows That Speak

In the garden, shadows play,
Hiding secrets, night and day.
They giggle as they dance around,
Whispering tales without a sound.

One shadow stole a gardener's hat,
Claimed it looked like a funny cat.
With a laugh, it tiptoed away,
Leaving behind a sunny ray.

Nature's Soft Confidants

Leaves are gossiping on the breeze,
Sharing stories with utmost ease.
A squirrel overheard a tree
Saying, "Look how spry I can be!"

Flowers chuckle when bumblebees
Tickle their petals, oh such tease!
Even the grass has a good laugh,
Counting the raindrops to craft a path.

The Garden's Gentle Echo

In the garden, echoes jest,
Giggling fruits, they know the best.
A tomato said to a shy peapod,
"Wanna join me? Don't be a fraud!"

The carrots joined in a lively race,
Rolling around in their cozy space.
And the pumpkins cheered, full of mirth,
"Let's celebrate our side of Earth!"

Shadows of the Ancient Trees

Old trees bend and sway with grace,
Throwing shadows, a playful space.
One wise branch murmurs to the next,
"Did you hear? That fox is perplexed!"

The roots rumble beneath the ground,
Exchanging jokes that swirl around.
One had a punchline, strong and bold,
"Why do we hide? It never gets old!"

Harmony in the Hedge

In the hedges, secrets thrive,
A squirrel plays, always alive.
Rabbits hop and chatter loud,
Making mischief in the crowd.

A fox rolls over, plays coy,
While a hedgehog bounces with joy.
Leaves giggle as they dance;
Nature's little, silly prance.

A snicker from the buzzing bee,
Tells a joke, just wait and see.
'Why do flowers never loaf?'
'Because they always need to grow, off!'

In this patch, laughter is free,
Joyous shouts from the old oak tree.
Nature's laughter fills the air,
Come join the fun, if you dare!

Essence of the Arboretum

In the grove, there's quite a scene,
A line of ants dressed in green.
They march with purpose, what a sight,
Trying to lift a leaf so bright.

A cactus jokes, 'I'm quite the prick,
But trust me, I'll give you a kick!'
The flowers giggle, colors bright,
'You'll need a friend to share your plight.'

A parrot squawks a riddle loud,
'The best dance? The one in the cloud!'
The trees sway side to side,
As if showing off their pride.

So come and tease the boughs today,
Laugh along with nature's play.
In this place, life's never grim,
Embrace the charm on a whim!

The Calm Beneath the Canopy

Beneath the leaves, a squirrel naps,
Dreaming of cheese and funny traps.
The calm is rich, the humor flows,
As vines tangle in funny shows.

A wise old owl hoots with glee,
'What did the tree say to me?'
'You're looking quite un-fern-gettable!'
His friends all chuckle, so relatable!

The ferns sway softly in the breeze,
Telling ticklish tales with ease.
A flower pipes up, 'What's so grand?
Life's better when we all stand hand in hand!'

In this dome, silliness blooms,
With laughter dancing amidst the glooms.
So gather round, come share a laugh,
In the green haven's heart, life's joy is daft!

Whispers Beneath the Willow

Under willows, whispers low,
A frog croaks jokes, giving a show.
'Why did the pine tree never play?'
'It couldn't find its way to sway!'

The old willow sways with mirth,
Says, 'I've seen all sorts of birth!'
From acorns to blossoms, each has a tale,
Including those that go off the rail!

A rabbit laughs 'Oh, what a mess!
I tried to dress in a flowered dress!'
Snakes curl up, they can't contain,
Their giggles echo through the rain.

So gather 'round, share a jest,
Nature's humor is truly the best.
In this grove, let spirits rise,
With cheerful whispers and friends, no lies!

Soothing Songs from the Soil

In the garden, worms sing low,
Chasing rumors of the crow.
Rabbits giggle, making tea,
While ants do the cha-cha, can't you see?

Under leaves, the beetles dance,
Spinning tales with a merry prance.
Mice have parties, cheese in sight,
But sneak away at the first moonlight.

The flowers chuckle, petals bright,
Sharing secrets in delight.
They whisper jokes at the buzzing bees,
Who forget their lines with the rustling breeze.

As the sun dips, the shadows play,
Saying, "Let's dance till the end of the day!"
The grasshoppers strum on a twig,
And every seed dreams of being big!

Harmonies of the Hidden Grove

In a nook where the breezes tease,
Mushrooms trade their jokes with ease.
Squirrels juggling acorns by,
While wise old owls let out a sigh.

Frogs croak choruses so absurd,
Competing with the chirping bird.
Every leaf has a strange tune,
Swaying gently beneath the moon.

The thorns claim they're just misunderstood,
While daisies flaunt their cheerful wood.
Vines tangle up in a silly knot,
As the sunbeams give it all they've got.

In this grove, life's a playful jest,
With laughter echoing through the nest.
So come, dear friend, just take a peek,
At nature's giggle — oh, so unique!

Garden Secrets

In the patch where gnomes reside,
Secrets sprout with every stride.
Roses tease the daisies bright,
"Try to dance, you're just too tight!"

Radishes plan an underground show,
While carrots play peek-a-boo in a row.
The sunflower lifts its head up high,
Winking at clouds that drift on by.

Caterpillars chat about their dreams,
Of turning into stars, at least it seems.
But pruning shears come and take a bite,
Making all their plans take flight!

So if you stroll through this leafy land,
You'll hear the giggles, oh so grand.
Nature's whispers are full of fun,
In a place where every leaf can run.

The Silent Grove

In the grove where giggles hide,
The tall trees have a silly side.
Branches twist in a funny way,
And start a dance at the break of day.

Mushrooms pull pranks, popping up quick,
Sprinkling laughs with a comedic trick.
While hedgehogs roll in a merry race,
Competing to see who can take first place.

Bugs wearing hats twirl a quick jig,
While a snail boasts of his giant gig.
The breeze carries tales from root to bough,
Echoing laughter at every how.

So explore this place where joy abounds,
A sanctuary filled with silly sounds.
In every nook, a chuckle's kept,
In this silent grove, laughter's leapt!

Secrets of the Stems

In leafy haunts, they giggle low,
With secrets only roots can know.
A flower blinks, then gives a wink,
Did that petal just nibble a drink?

The daisies whisper, 'What's the buzz?'
While dandelions roll like fuzz.
A tulip blushes, red and bright,
'Oh dear, I forgot—it's my big night!'

The mint is minty, makes us grin,
While beetles dance in leaf's soft skin.
A cactus jokes, 'I'm prickly nice!'
But really, I'm your dessert slice!'

Gather 'round for laughter's cheer,
Among the stems, there's no fear.
In nature's jest, we all partake,
Even the mushrooms know to shake!

The Gentle Tones of Tansy

In fields of gold, the tansy sings,
Of ladybugs and fluttering wings.
'Watch my dance, I twirl and spin!'
Said one sweet bloom—let chaos begin!

The bumblebees join in the fray,
Their buzzing chorus in fine display.
While petals toss like hats in glee,
A stubborn weed shouts, 'Look at me!'

'The sun is hot, let's grab a seat!'
Said the clover, all spruced and neat.
With gentle tunes and laughter bright,
They sway through blissful, sunny light.

So gather close, my flowery friends,
Where good times bloom, the fun never ends.
Upon the breeze, let your joy bounce,
In every swish, let the giggles pounce!

Quietude Under the Quercus

Beneath the oak, they tell their tales,
Of acorns falling like tiny sails.
'I missed the catch!' shouts a squirrel bold,
While laughter rings through leaves of gold.

The shadows play their quiet games,
As critters dance with silly names.
A fern reports, 'What's with the fuss?'
There's always drama on the bus!

The moss is soft, a cozy bed,
With whispers that make daisies red.
A chipmunk naps, but gives a cheer,
'This shady spot, the best right here!'

So if you seek some humor sweet,
Just pause and listen, find your seat.
Under the quercus, life's a jest,
Nature's giggles, truly the best!

The Lifting Leaves

The leaves erupt in joyful throngs,
Swaying gently to nature's songs.
'Catch me, wind!' they cheer and shout,
While twirling round without a doubt!

The cherries laugh as they sway high,
'Just look at us, we're so spry!'
With every breeze, the fun reveals,
A game of tag among the seals.

A banana peel slides, oh-so slick,
'Whoa there!' yells a playful chick.
But nature's laughter, it won't cease,
As all join in, embracing peace.

So lift your heart with nature's glee,
In every leaf, a shimm'ring spree.
For in the rustle, we find our highs,
In every giggle, beneath blue skies!

www.ingramcontent.com/pod-product-compliance
Lightning Source LLC
Chambersburg PA
CBHW070315120526
44590CB00017B/2692